Focus on History

edited by Ray Mitchell and Geoffrey Middleton

The Transport Revolution

Roger Watson

CUCKFIELD

RYEGATE

COMET
BRIGHTON
&
LONDON

Longman

Travellers in the early eighteenth century

If you were making a journey in the early part of the eighteenth century, what would you have seen on the roads?

This picture was drawn in France, but in England you would have seen the same sights. Pick out:

– two men walking and carrying sacks on their backs.

– a lady on a horse with her shopping basket.

– a two-wheeled cart drawn by one horse.

– an open four-wheeled wagon carrying sacks of something.

  What could be in them?

– a covered wagon with people inside.

Now look at the road. How does it differ from roads today? Has the surface been specially made? Does it follow a clearly marked track?

The picture shows how most people travelled at this time. Do you think that many of them would have made long journeys like this, or would they have kept to their own towns and villages?

One group of people who did have to make long journeys were the traders, such as the wool merchants. How did they manage? The picture above shows the commonest way of sending goods about the country. Look at the horse. It is called a *packhorse* because it carries a pack or bundle of goods on its back. Packhorses were used to carry all sorts of goods. Notice the path. Is it specially made?

There were also huge wagons which carried goods and people between some important towns. Here is a picture of one. Can you see
— the very broad wheels? Why did it need these?
— how many horses are pulling it?
— the wagon master with his long whip? What does this tell you about the speed at which the wagon could travel?
— what it is doing to the road?

Cattle, sheep, geese and turkeys were also driven in large herds (called *droves*) to market, since this was the only way to get them there.

The picture shows a drove road in the Highlands of Scotland. Can you see the herds of sheep and cattle, with the *drovers* in the foreground and their dogs? Notice that the artist painted the drovers with bare feet.

Huge numbers of cattle and sheep were moved like this. Can you imagine what these millions of hooves did to the soft roads?

If you were quite well off, you could travel between some of the large towns by public stage-coach. The very wealthy had their own coaches. Look at this advertisement for the Birmingham stage-coach. Can you read it? Sometimes the letter s is printed as an f. Find out from your atlas how far Birmingham is from London. Then, can you work out the average speed the coach travelled? Remember that the coach travelled all night. You will have to guess what time it arrived. Can you also work out how much it cost in old pence per mile or kilometre?

BIRMINGHAM STAGE-COACH,

In Two *Days* and a half; begins *May* the 24th, '1731.

SET Sout from the *Swan-Inn* in *Birmingham*, every *Monday* at fix a Clock in the Morning, through *Warwick*, *Banbury* and *Alesbury*, to the *Red Lion Inn* in *Alderfgate ftreet*, *London*, every *Wednefday* Morning: And returns from the faid *Red Lion Inn* every *Thurfday* Morning at five a Clock the fame Way to the *Swan-Inn* in *Birmingham* every *Saturday*, at 21 Shillings each Paffenger, and 18 Shillings from *Warwick*, who has liberty to carry 14 Pounds in Weight, and all above to *pay One Penny a Pound*.

Perform d (if God permit)

By Nicholas Rothwell.

It is difficult to compare the cost of travel then with travel now because money was worth so much more then. It is best to compare the cost of travel with the cost of other things at the same time. In the mid-eighteenth century a farm labourer might earn 7 shillings a week and a skilled man twice that. A 4 lb. (approx. 2 kg.) loaf of bread cost 5 pence.

The picture below is by William Hogarth, a famous eighteenth century artist. It shows a stage-coach loading in the courtyard of an inn. Notice that there are no windows in the coach. Can you see the passengers perched on top, and the lady in the basket at the back which is mainly for luggage? You could travel more cheaply in these positions, but would it have been comfortable?

In this book we are going to find out how travel changed after the early eighteenth century. To keep track of the changes you will need to make a big time-chart. Get some large sheets of paper and stick them edge to edge with sellotape to make one long piece. Along the bottom mark the dates from 1700 every 5 years to 1900. Begin your time-chart by drawing a packhorse and a stage-coach between the marks for 1700 and 1725. One can go above the other so that you can draw them quite large. Mark the speed of the Birmingham stage coach against your drawing.

Roads in the eighteenth century

In 1770 Arthur Young wrote a description of the road from Preston
to Wigan. He warned travellers that 'They will meet here with ruts,
which I actually measured four feet deep (120 cm) and floating with
mud only from a wet summer; what therefore must it be after winter?
The only mending it received is the tumbling in of some loose stones.'

Roads were so bad at this time that many could not be used in the
winter at all. This was because nobody really understood how to make
roads suitable for wheeled traffic. When bad holes appeared they were
filled with loose stones. Above is a picture by an eighteenth century
artist Thomas Bewick. It shows a workman breaking stones to repair
the road with. What kind of tools is he using? After a bit the wheels
just squashed these stones into the mud and there was a hole again.

To stop this, laws were passed to make wagons use broader wheels.
Look again at the wagon on page 3. The picture below advertised a
wagon which even ran on rollers. Can you think of the snag in this
idea? If you count the number of horses it will give you a clue.

Another problem was that each parish had to mend its own roads. Most people in the parish had to work 4 or 6 days on the roads each year, or pay money instead. Not surprisingly, they disliked this and shirked the work.

During the eighteenth century a new system developed. Groups of men agreed to keep a stretch of road in good repair if they could charge a fee or *toll* to everyone who used the road. They put barriers called *turnpikes* across the road to stop travellers until they had paid the toll. Usually a tollhouse was built beside the barrier for the man who collected the tolls. Look at this picture of a tollgate. Can you pick out the tollhouse, the gates and the tollkeeper? What sort of people are using the tollgate? Many of these tollhouses still exist.

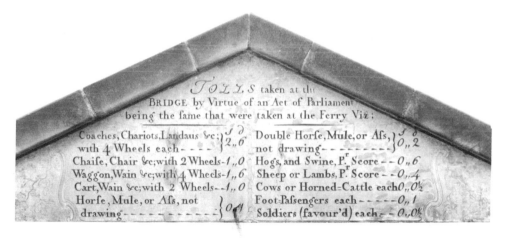

You cannot see the list of tolls in the top picture, but probably it would have been like this one at a tollbridge in Leicestershire. How much would the people in the picture above have to pay if the tolls at that gate were the same as for the bridge? The sheep are difficult to count and you may have to look up some words in your dictionary.

A stage-coach journey

The Turnpike System improved the roads, and by the 1780s coaches could travel more quickly and comfortably.

Parson Woodforde described a stage-coach journey at this time in his diary. He went from Norwich to London and then on to Bath.

Here is his account:

June 23. At 7 o'clock this Evening, myself, Nancy and Brother went in the heavy coach for London. For 3 Peoples Fare to London I pd. £4. 10. 0. For extra luggage — 12 st. I paid 0. 15. 0. It was very hot this evening, especially with a coach full.

June 24. We had a very pleasant night of travelling. We went thro' Bury etc. We breakfasted very early but where I know not — I paid for our breakfasts 0. 3. 0. To the Coachman who drove us half way gave 0. 3. 0. We all got to London (thank God) safe and well by 3 o'clock this afternoon . . . To the last Coachman gave 0. 3. 0. . . . to our old Inn the Bell Savage at Ludgate Hill where we supped and slept.

June 25. Very much pestered and bit by the Buggs in the night.

June 26. I was bit so terribly by Buggs again this night that I got up at 4 o'clock this morning and took a long walk by myself about the City till Breakfast time.

June 27. For three Places in the Bath Coach for tomorrow Night, for part of the fare thither pd. 3. 3. 0. . . . I did not pull of my Cloaths last night but sat up in a great chair all night with my feet up on the bed and slept very well considering and not pestered with buggs.

This stage-coach was in use about the time of Parson Woodforde's journey. Can you see
— which inn it is leaving?
— how many outside passengers there are?
— where they are sitting?
— how many horses there are?

June 28. I paid at the Bell Savage our Bill 3.14.0. To servants at the Inn gave 0.10.6. At a qr. before 7 this evening Nancy and self got into the Bath Coach.

June 29. About 4 o'clock this morning we all breakfasted but at what place I know not — pd. for the same 0.4.0. To the first Coach-man and Guard I gave 0.4.0. For the other part of our Fare to Bath pd. 1.7.0. For extra luggage — pd. also at breakfast 0.13.0. We all got safe to Bath (thank God) this morning about 10 o'clock.'

Use this account and an atlas to work out:

— the average speed of the coach from Norwich to Bath including the time taken over meals.

— the cost in pence per mile or kilometre from Norwich to Bath.

Draw this stage-coach on your time-chart and mark its speed on your drawing.

By this time a farm labourer might earn 9 or 10 shillings a week and a skilled man twice as much. A 4 lb. (approx. 2 kg.) loaf cost 7 pence.

Here is a mail-coach ticket. Can you find out:
— when it was issued?
— where?
— for what journey?
— how much the journey cost?
— how this compares with the cost of Parson Woodforde's journey?

The mail-coach revolution

This is a picture of a postboy. He is carrying the mail in the leather wallet slung at his side, and is blowing his horn. This was a warning to open the tollgates so that the post would not have to stop. The post did not have to pay tolls.

The post had been carried on horseback for hundreds of years. But by the late eighteenth century stage-coaches could travel much faster. A coach could go from London to Bristol in 17 hours while the postboy took 38 hours.

John Palmer of Bath thought that if the mail was sent by coach it would be quicker, safer and cheaper because the coaches could carry passengers too. At first the Post Office was not interested in his idea, but he kept badgering them and in 1784 he was allowed to start a mail-coach service between London and Bristol at his own expense.

This picture below shows the very first mail-coach. Pick out:
— the coachman
— the guard with his shotgun
— the passengers
— the royal coat of arms
— the words 'Bath and Bristol Mail'
Draw this mail-coach on your time-chart and mark it 'First mail-coach 1784'.

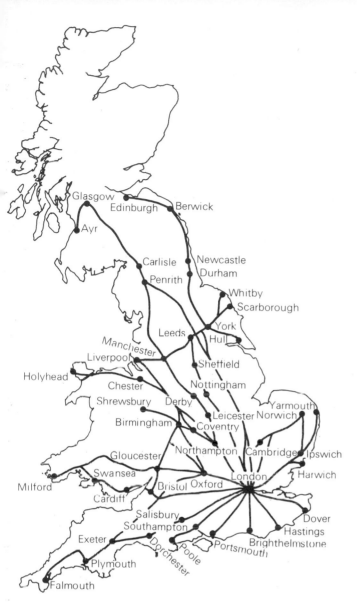

John Palmer's mail-coach was an immediate success. At this time trade was growing quickly. So businessmen needed to send letters all over the country and get quick replies. Because Palmer's mail-coach gave this service more routes were soon added.

This map shows the main mail-coach routes in 1800. Notice how they start from London and spread out to the main towns.

The design of the mail-coaches was improved too. Below is a picture of the standard mail-coach. How does it differ from the first mail-coach opposite? Notice:

— the guard blowing his horn. The mail is in the box under his feet.
— how many passengers can be seen?
— the initials of the reigning monarch. W stands for the name and R for Rex, the Latin word for King. Will this help you to date the picture?
— the tollgate on the bridge in the background.

The horses which pulled the mail-coaches were changed several times on the journey and the coaches ran to a very strict timetable. This picture shows a time-bill. Each coach carried one, and it had to be filled in by the guard and sent back to the Post Office in London at the end of each journey.

Can you find out from the time-bill:
— where the coach stopped to change horses?
— how long was allowed for changing horses?
— if there were any stops for meals?
— how long the journey took? How does this compare with Parson Woodforde's journey. If the coach was late the guard had to explain why.

The guard's watch was locked so that he could not disguise his time of arrival. Soon people began to say that you could set your watch by the mail-coaches.

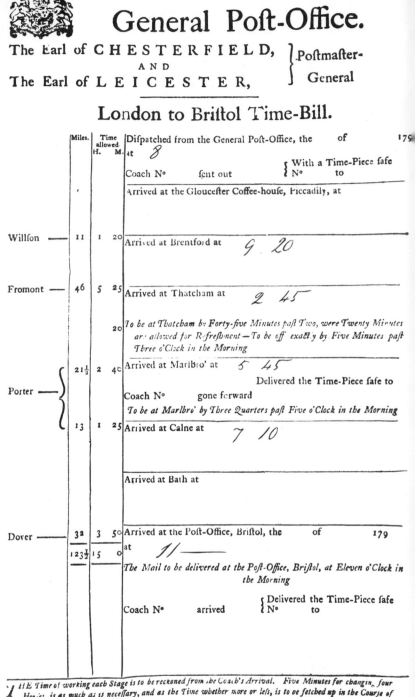

General Post-Office.

The Earl of CHESTERFIELD, }
AND } Postmaster-General
The Earl of LEICESTER, }

London to Bristol Time-Bill.

	Miles	Time allowed H. M.	
			Dispatched from the General Post-Office, the of 179
			at 8
			Coach No sent out { With a Time-Piece safe No to
			Arrived at the Gloucester Coffee-house, Piccadily, at
Willson	11	1 20	Arrived at Brentford at 9 20
Fromont	46	5 25	Arrived at Thatcham at 2 45
		20	To be at Thatcham by Forty-five Minutes past Two, were Twenty Minutes are allowed for Refreshment — To be off exactly by Five Minutes past Three o'Clock in the Morning
Porter {	21½	2 40	Arrived at Marlbro' at 5 45
			Delivered the Time-Piece safe to
			Coach No gone forward
			To be at Marlbro' by Three Quarters past Five o'Clock in the Morning
	13	1 25	Arrived at Calne at 7 10
			Arrived at Bath at
Dover	32	3 50	Arrived at the Post-Office, Bristol, the of 179
	123½	15 0	at 11
			The Mail to be delivered at the Post-Office, Bristol, at Eleven o'Clock in the Morning
			Coach No arrived { Delivered the Time-Piece safe No to

THE Time of working each Stage is to be reckoned from the Coach's Arrival. Five Minutes for changing four Horses, is as much as is necessary, and as the Time whether more or less, is to be fetched up in the Course of the Stage, it is the Coachman's Duty to be as expeditious as possible, and to report the Horse-keepers if they are not always ready when the Coach arrives, and active in getting it off.

By Command of the Postmaster-General,

T. HASKER.

It must have been a tough job keeping the mails moving in winter. This picture shows a coach which has got stuck in the snow. When this happened it was the guard's job to get the mail on to the next stop. Can you see him riding off on one of the horses? What are the other men doing? Think how cold it must have been for outside passengers in winter. One or two actually froze to death. Imagine that you are a passenger in this coach and describe your adventure in getting to the next inn.

By 1825 the mail business was so big that a huge new Post Office had to be built in London. Every night the mail-coaches for different parts of the country set out from it all together. Look at the time-bill opposite and find out at what time they started. It must have been a fine sight. Draw your own picture of a mail-coach and paint it in the correct colours — maroon for the lower part of the body, black for the upper parts and red for the wheels.

Two great road builders

The fast running mail- and stage-coaches needed better roads. In the early 1800s two great road builders began to provide them.

The best known is John Macadam, a Scotsman who was made Highway Surveyor in Bristol in 1816. This is his portrait. Macadam's method of making and repairing roads worked so well that soon he was being consulted by turnpike trusts all over the country.

Macadam realised that ordinary ground will carry almost any weight if it is dry. His roads were designed to keep the ground dry. Look at this diagram to see how he did it. Do you see how the road is curved a little from the centre to the edges? How did this help? On top of the earth Macadam laid three layers of small broken stones. In the bottom two layers the stones had to be of about the same size and weigh not more than six ounces (170 g). The top layer sometimes had smaller stones. The coach wheels packed these stones down tight and broke off a fine grit which bound the surface together. After a while water would run off the surface and not wet the soil underneath.

John Macadam

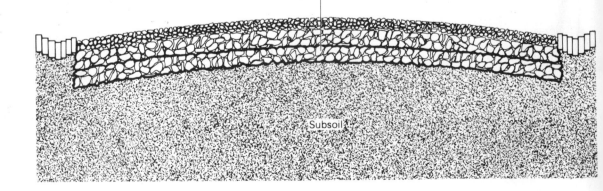

three layers of broken stones

Subsoil

The other great road builder at this time was another Scotsman, Thomas Telford. Here is a portrait of him.

The diagram below shows how Telford built roads. Compare this with the diagram showing Macadam's method. How do the two methods differ? Both men agreed that a road must be well drained. Do you see the curve of the road (called *camber*) in each diagram? The main difference is that Telford liked to build his roads on a solid foundation. Look at the big stones in the bottom layer. These were laid carefully by hand. Smaller, broken stones were then put on, so that the whole foundation was packed solid. On top of this came further layers of small broken stones, and sometimes a layer of gravel on top. Can you imagine how long it took to build roads like this? It was certainly a much more expensive method than Macadam's but Telford built his roads to last.

Make a model of Telford and Macadam's methods using gravel and small stones.

Thomas Telford

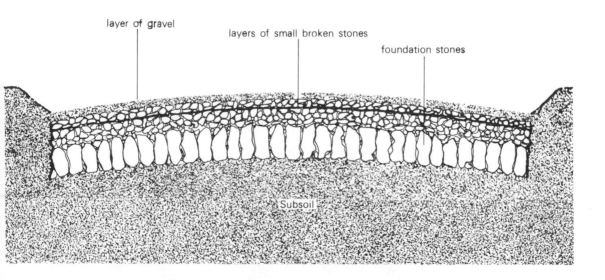

layer of gravel

layers of small broken stones

foundation stones

Subsoil

This picture shows Telford driving in the Highlands of Scotland where he did his greatest road building. Is there anything in the picture to show that this is in Scotland? Towards the end of the eighteenth century the Highlands were in a bad way. Many people were being turned off the land so that the lairds (landowners) could keep sheep there instead. In 1801 Telford was asked to make a survey of the Highlands and say what could be done to improve communications there. He recommended several harbours to encourage the fishing industry, a canal through the Great Glen (page 34), and a big programme of road building so that people and goods could move more freely.

The Government agreed to Telford's proposals and he was put in charge of this huge project. During the next eighteen years he was responsible for the building of 920 miles (1,470 km) of new roads, and over one thousand bridges. Can you imagine what a difficult job it was building all these roads and bridges in such a remote part of the country? One of Telford's assistants on this job walked 5,000 miles (8,000 km) in one year alone.

As well as his Highland roads Telford was also asked to improve the road from London to Holyhead so that the mail to Ireland could get through more quickly. Look back at the map on page 11. What route did the mail-coaches take from London to Holyhead? Is it the most direct route?

Telford built a new road from Shrewsbury to Holyhead — the A5 in
your atlas. Here is one of the bridges which he built on the new road.
It is at Bettws-Y-Coed in Wales and is still in use today. Can you tell
in which year it was built?

He also had to bridge the Menai Straits to carry the road to
Holyhead on the island of Anglesey. Can you see the chains which run
over the tops of two towers? The roadway is hung or suspended from
these chains and so the bridge is called a suspension bridge. It was
opened in 1826 and was the first really large suspension bridge to be
built. Mark the date on your time-chart. Notice that in both these
bridges Telford used iron. In what ways do you think iron is better than
stone for building bridges? Make a model of the bridge with balsawood,
string and cardboard. Where do you think the ends of the chains
would be fixed?

The golden age of coaching

With better roads and the mail-coaches setting the pace, coaching was at its best in the early part of the nineteenth century. Fast coaches travelled to most parts of the country. Here is a picture of one of them. It is called the 'Comet' and ran between London and Brighton in six hours in the early 1820s. Can you see the name on the coach and a tollgate in the distance? Notice how well dressed the passengers are. Brighton at this time was the smartest place in the country. Find the passenger sitting next to the coachman. This was a favourite place, because sometimes the coachman would let you take over the reins, though this was against the law. How many other passengers are there travelling outside? Look up in your atlas the place names written on the coach and you will see what route it took. How does the 'Comet's' speed compare with Parson Woodforde's coach forty years earlier? Draw the 'Comet' on your time-chart and add its speed.

The inns too had improved since Parson Woodforde was so badly
bitten by bugs. In 1827 a visiting Italian wrote: 'At every inn on the
road, breakfast, dinner, or supper is always ready, a fire is burning in
every room and water always boiling for tea or coffee. Soft feather
beds, with a fire blazing up the chimney, invite to repose; and the
tables are covered with newspapers for the amusement of the
passengers.'

Look at this picture of passengers having breakfast at the Bull Inn,
Redbourn, Hertfordshire, on the Holyhead road. This was a rather
grand inn and it certainly looks comfortable. Pick out:
— the coachman with his long whip and heavy coat
— two men thawing out by the fire
— a man being shaved
— the guard outside blowing his horn because it is time to get back
  to the coach.

Of course, this was still a very expensive way to travel, and only the
well-off could afford it, but these pictures can help us to understand
why people call this 'the golden age of coaching'.

Carrying heavy goods

Stage-coaches and better roads had certainly made travel easier for people. But heavy goods remained a problem. In 1722 Daniel Defoe had described how difficult it was to get trees to Chatham for the shipbuilders.

'I have seen one tree on a carriage, which they here call a tug, drawn by two and twenty oxen, and even then, 'tis carried so little a way, and then thrown down, and left for other tugs to take up and carry on, that sometimes 'tis two or three years before it gets to Chatham: for if once the rains come in it stirs no more that year.'

Most people who had heavy goods to move sent them by water. Rivers such as the Thames, Severn and Trent have been busy with traffic since the earliest times. Unfortunately, the water in these rivers was not always deep enough and barges might be stranded for weeks in a dry summer.

The picture shows one of the earliest methods of solving this problem. It is called a *flash-lock* and is a man-made barrier across the river. The water built up behind this barrier, and barges could travel safely in the deeper water. But how did barges get past the flash-locks? Can you see the long-handled paddle which the man is pulling up? Each of these paddles had to be pulled out and the barge then floated down on the *flush* or *flash* of water which was released. That is why it is called a flash-lock.

20

Flash-locks helped to make the rivers more navigable. But it was slow work getting past them and they wasted a lot of water. The picture above shows a different kind of lock. Can you see a *weir* half way along the main channel of the river? This is a permanent barrier in the river. To the left of this is a man-made channel called a *cut*. At the near end of the cut is a lock with a pair of gates at each end of a stretch of water. If you look carefully you can see a mast sticking up between the two gates. This is called a *pound-lock*. Write a paragraph with diagrams to explain how you think this lock worked. Look at page 27 if you find this difficult. Do you think it was better than the flash-lock?

This busy scene is St. Katharine's Dock, London in the early 1800s. Pick out:
— the sailing ships
— the goods piled on the quayside
— the warehouses in the background.
Some of these still exist.
Goods had been sent by sea round the coast of Britain for a long time. Coal was being shipped from Newcastle to London in 1299. It was often called sea-coal. In the seventeenth and eighteenth centuries coastal shipping grew enormously.

The Bridgewater Canal

As business grew in the North and the Midlands there was a need for waterways where no rivers flowed. It is a short step from improving a river with cuts and locks to cutting an artificial river or canal. In 1757 the first such canal in England was built — the Sankey Canal. It ran from the St. Helen's coalfield to the Mersey River and was used to supply Liverpool with coal. Two years later work started on a much more important project — the Bridgewater Canal.

The picture above shows where this canal started. Can you see the two little tunnels in the rockface? These led straight into the Duke of Bridgewater's coal mine at Worsley. The Duke had found that it was very expensive taking the coal by packhorse to nearby Manchester, so he planned to build a canal there from his mine. He was helped by John Gilbert, the land agent who looked after the Bridgewater Estates, and James Brindley, a local man, who was recommended to the Duke as a very clever engineer, though he had never been to school.

Can you see the boats in the foreground? These were used to carry coal out from the coalface. Because these boats were so narrow they were called 'starvationers'.

Here is a portrait of James Brindley. What has the artist drawn in the background? The instrument beside Brindley is called a theodolite. You can still see road-makers with instruments like this today. Try to find out what they are used for.

Gilbert and Brindley planned to build the canal all on one level. To do this they had to cross the River Irwell at Barton. This picture shows how they did it. This special bridge is called an aqueduct. It carries the waters of the canal over the river. Can you see the barge being pulled across by two horses? How can you tell that there was a path beside the canal?

When this aqueduct was first built people came from all over the country to look at it. Arthur Young was one who came to look, and was amazed by:

'The effect of coming on to Barton Bridge, and looking down upon a large river with barges . . . sailing on it; and up to another river, hung in the air, with barges towing along it.'

The Bridgewater Canal was opened in 1761 and was a great success. The Duke was able to sell coal in Manchester for half the price he had charged before, and as a result he sold more and more of it. Draw a picture of the Barton aqueduct on your time-chart and mark the date when the Bridgewater Canal opened. Was it built before the main road improvements?

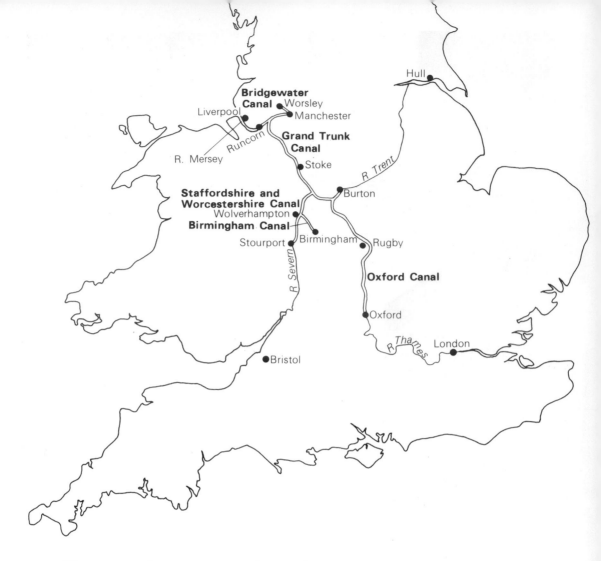

The canal system takes shape

The Bridgewater Canal was not the first in England, but it is important because it was the start of a whole system of canals. The Duke was pleased with his first canal to Manchester, and planned to extend it 35 miles (56 km) to meet the Mersey Estuary at Runcorn. Other men also began to plan canals, and James Brindley was called in to supervise most of them.

Look at this map and pick out:
— the Bridgewater Canal
— the Trent and Mersey Canal which Brindley called the 'Grand Trunk'.
Which two rivers does this join?
— the Oxford Canal
— the Staffordshire and Worcestershire Canal
— the Birmingham Canal.

Can you see how this system of canals makes a cross which links four great rivers and their main ports? Make a list of these rivers and ports. What was the advantage of this canal system for businessmen?

One of the first businessmen to realise what a help canals could be was Josiah Wedgwood, the famous pottery owner. He put up much of the money for the Trent and Mersey Canal. Above is the new pottery works which he built on the banks of that canal at Burslem in Staffordshire. Find the loading dock with a small crane. Notice the barge in the foreground and compare it with the barge on page 23. What difference can you see? When the canal was built Wedgwood could ship china clay from Cornwall to Liverpool and then along the canal to his pottery. At the same time his fragile pottery and china could go by barge to Liverpool or Hull. Before, it had had to go by packhorse or wagon. Why do you think Wedgwood was ready to spend money on this canal?

Brindley died from overwork in 1772 before he could see his great schemes completed. But by then canals were accepted, and more and more were being built. By 1830 there were 4,000 miles (6,400 km) of canals which served all the main industrial areas of the country.

How the canals were built

Here is an estimate of the cost of making a small canal. Use it to find out what the two most expensive jobs on the canal were. Draw a diagram to show the shape of a cross-section of the canal. Why do you think it was built like this?

An Estimate of the Expense of making a Navigable Canal from Lord Dudleys Tunnel in the parish of Tipton in the County of Stafford, to join the Dudley Canal at Netherton in the County of Worcester.

The whole length of this canal is 1. 7. 4. 00, of which one mile and five furlongs must be Tunnelled, and two furlongs four chains is open cutting.

The Tunnel to be 14 feet high and 9 feet wide, to stand five feet deep in Water. The open Canal to be 20 feet wide at top Water and 16 feet wide at the bottom, and to stand 4 feet 6 inches deep in Water.

	£	s	d
To 1 mile 5 furlongs of Tunnelling at 5. 5. 0 per yard forward including temporary damages done to Land supervising &c, and also including one stop Lock	15015	0	0
To 159 yards long of cutting at the West end of the Tunnel including benching the same	205	17	3
To 369 yards of level cutting at 4" per yard forward	73	16	0
To 1 bridge	70	0	0
To 31 feet of Lockage at 60£ per foot	1860	0	0
To 1 acre 3 rood of Land at 40£ per acre	70	0	0
To 66 perch of gravelling the Towing path and fencing the same at 12" per perch	39	12	0
To Temporary damages done to Land, supervising &c 15£ per cent on the open part of the Canal	359	17	9
	17274	3	0

26

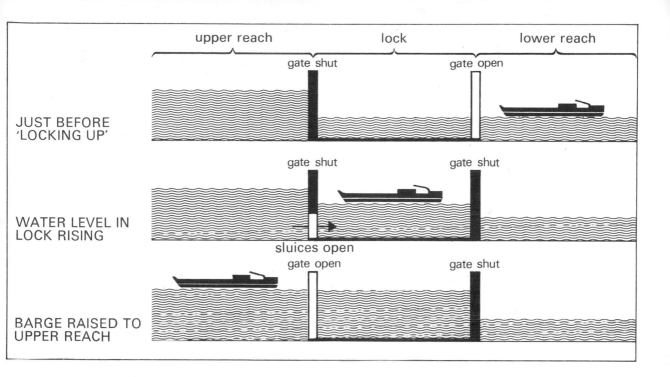

upper reach   lock   lower reach

JUST BEFORE 'LOCKING UP' — gate shut, gate open

WATER LEVEL IN LOCK RISING — gate shut, gate shut

BARGE RAISED TO UPPER REACH — sluices open, gate open, gate shut

Keeping a canal filled with water was often very difficult. When possible the engineer would make streams run into the canal. If there were no streams he would have to build a *reservoir* at the high point of the canal to supply it. Can you think why canals needed so much water? To stop the water seeping out, the canal was lined with *puddled* clay. This is clay which has been kneaded with water until it becomes waterproof. Try making some yourself.

Where possible, Brindley made his canals follow one level. This made them very twisty but fairly cheap to build. When the canal had to go up or down hill he used 'pound-locks' such as were already in use on the rivers (page 21). The diagram above shows how a pound-lock works. Now do you see why canals needed so much water?

If the canal had to go up a steep hill several locks were joined together to form a *staircase*. Here is one at Foxton in Leicestershire. Would barges be able to pass each other?

Staircase locks were slow in use and needed vast quantities of water. Some engineers tried to replace them with huge lifts. Here is one which was built at Foxton in 1900. Can you see the two barges which have been floated into a large steel box called a *caisson*? The caisson with the barges in it is being pulled on wheels up the rails to the next level of canal. Today there is only one lift in use — the Anderton lift near Northwich in Cheshire.

When a canal engineer was faced with a very large hill to pass he would arrange to tunnel through it. James Brindley started the first great canal tunnel — the Harecastle Tunnel on the Trent and Mersey Canal. It was over a mile and a half (2½ km) long and took eleven years to build. The diagram shows you how these long tunnels were built. Workmen started from each end, and from the bottom of the upright shafts which were sunk on the line of the tunnel. Make a picture of a tunnel being built. Show the working shaft with a big bucket to lift men and rubble, workmen with pickaxes and candles for light and dynamite being used to break up the rocks.

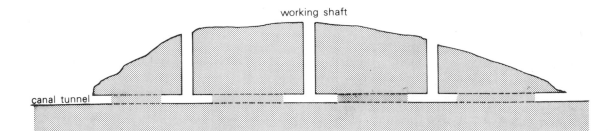

working shaft

canal tunnel

Here is the inside of Blisworth Tunnel on the Grand Junction Canal. Notice the brick lining to the tunnel, and the fact that there is no towpath. How do you think barges got through in the years before they were fitted with engines?

Hills were difficult for canals to cross but river valleys were almost as bad. Usually the engineers did as Gilbert and Brindley had done on the Bridgewater Canal and built an aqueduct. Probably the finest aqueduct is the Pont Cysyllte (pronounced 'Kersulty') built by Telford, near Llangollen. Here is a modern photograph of it. Compare it with the Barton aqueduct on page 23. Can you see the stone pillars and the cast iron channel at the top which carries the water? Telford invented this method because a canal in its puddled clay bed would have been far too heavy for the pillars at that great height. Where do you think he put the towpath? The aqueduct took ten years to build and was opened in 1805. It is over 1,000 feet (300 metres) long and the stone pillars carry the canal 127 feet (38 metres) above the River Dee (five times as high as a house). Draw a picture of it for your time-chart. Boats can still cross this aqueduct today.

Life and work on the canals

In the early days most canal companies were not allowed to carry goods in their own barges. People were afraid that this would make the companies too powerful, and that they would then be able to charge high prices. So the canals worked like the roads and boatmen had to pay tolls for using them.

Boats were usually worked by two men or a man and a boy. Later, when competition from the railways drove down boatmen's pay, the whole family took to living on the boat. This drawing of a family in a boat was made in 1874. What are they doing? What has the wife got on her lap? The next page shows family boats which were in use until quite recently. The photograph at the top shows how cramped the living space was. Can you pick out:

— the stove with pans on it
— the collapsible table with cups and plates on it
— the brass oil lamp
— hanging in front of fancy plates, three handles (called *windlasses*) for opening the sluices in locks. Find the sluices in the diagram of a lock on page 27.
— the family photographs?

You can see the cabin of a boat like this in the Waterways Museum at Stoke Bruerne, Northants.

Here is a boat being steered by the boatman's wife. Can you see the paintings on the end of the cabin? Notice the child. As boat families were always on the move the boat children seldom learned to read or write, though they learned to work the boats. Would you have liked to live on a canal boat? Try to imagine the life and write a letter to a friend explaining what it was like. Draw pictures of the boat to illustrate your letter.

Until the middle of the nineteenth century most canal boats were towed by horses. Here are some small boats being towed on the Rolle Canal in Devon. How many horses and men are there to work each boat? Can you see the aqueduct?

In the late eighteenth century people began to try using steam engines in boats, but the canal owners were afraid that the wash from the boats would damage the canal banks and these experiments were given up. Boats with steam engines only began to be used much after 1840 because of competition from the railways.

Here you see how boats were moved through tunnels that had no towpath. This boat is coming out of Blisworth Tunnel. The two men are called 'leggers'. What are they doing? Here is how an old boatman explained it: 'Legging? We put the boards out on each side of the boat, at the front, and fastened them there. Then we slipped a half sack of corn under as a cushion, see, and just walked our way along the sides of the tunnel, inside 'Arecastle that is, weaving our feet over each other, lying half sideways all the time. We just kept on walking! It took us about two hours and a half, and very damp it was too. Dripping damp and dark.' Later, steam tugs pulled the boats through.

Pleasure

And PACKET BOATS are daily starting from BATH and BRADFORD, on the Kennet and Avon Canal, in which Parties may enjoy a most delightful Ride, and beautiful Picturesque Scenery.

Without

The Inconvenience of Horse Exercise or Walking.
No Expence has been spared to render them Commodious, and remove every Idea of

Fatigue.

Terms and Hours of Starting may be known at the Boat Office, N.E. Side of Sydney Garden, or of Mr. Andras, Milsom-St.
GYE, Printer, MARKET-PLACE, Bath.

Mostly, the canals were used to shift heavy bulky goods. Can you think what goods would be most suitable for canals? Most of the canals were built in the industrial areas, and Birmingham became the most important canal centre.

Some canals did carry passengers as well as goods. Above is a poster advertising trips on the Kennet and Avon Canal. Read it and then explain in your own words what the advertisers thought passengers would like about their trip. Below is another picture of a canal boat crowded with passengers. Look carefully at the passengers. Do you think they were well off or ordinary working folk? Pick out the steersman and the thick rope at the left hand side. What do you think this goes to? Do you think people were likely to use these boats for regular travel or special trips?

Once railways had arrived canals lost all their passenger traffic. Today there is very little goods traffic on the canals but more and more people want to go on them for pleasure trips.

The ship canals

Because coastal shipping was so important there were several plans for ship canals which could save difficult or lengthy sea journeys. The map shows the most important ones which were actually built. The Crinan Canal was begun in 1793. This nine mile (14 km) canal saved a sea journey of 85 miles (136 km) round the Mull of Kintyre.

An even bigger project was the Caledonian Canal which was started in 1803 with Telford as engineer. The canal took nearly 20 years to finish, and was much the biggest engineering work in the country up to that time. Unfortunately, the Caledonian Canal was never used as much as Telford had hoped. Mainly, this was because the new steam ships which came into use after it was finished were soon being built too big to pass through the locks.

Both the Gloucester and Manchester Ship Canals were built to make those towns into ports. The River Severn below Gloucester was very treacherous for ships, and the canal was planned to link Gloucester with the deeper waters of the Severn. It also was started in 1793, and took 34 years to build, mainly because the company ran out of money. Once finished it was very successful, and is still in use today.

Here is the bed of the Manchester Ship Canal being dug out. It gives some idea how big a job it was. Notice how the soil is being taken away. This was the last great canal to be built in England. It was opened in 1894, and cost over £14 million pounds.

At one point the canal had to pass under the old Bridgewater Canal. To do this they had to pull down Brindley's Barton Aqueduct. In its place was built an amazing swing bridge. The picture below shows the opening of the canal. Can you see the swing bridge to the left of the ship with flags on? It has been swung round out of the way of the ships. It can be swung back across the ship canal to join up the Bridgewater canal. Draw this swing bridge on your time-chart and write a sentence about it.

The first railways

Look at this coal wagon. Can you pick out
— the rails it runs on? What do you think these are made of?
— the rim on the wheels, called a flange? What is this for?
— the brake with long curved handle? When would this be used?
— the colliery where the coal was produced?
— the jetty where wagons were emptied into the waiting ships?
Compare this load with the wagon on page 3. Why does the coal wagon need only one horse to pull it?

These coal wagon-ways were the first sort of railways and were built much earlier than the canals — from the seventeenth century onwards. Here is a description written by Daniel Defoe in 1726. He saw coals 'loaded into a great machine, called a Waggon, which by means of an artificial road, call'd a Waggon-way, goes with the help of but one horse . . . and this sometimes three or four miles to the nearest river.'

Draw a picture of a coal wagon at the beginning of your time-chart and underneath write a paragraph about these first railways. These first wooden wagon-ways were built to connect the coal mines of the North East to the Rivers Tyne and Wear. Later they spread to other parts of the country.

SURREY
Iron Railway.

The COMMITTEE of the SURREY IRON RAILWAY COMPANY,

HEREBY, GIVE NOTICE,. That the BASON at *Wandsworth*, and the Railway therefrom up to *Croydon* and *Carſhalton*, is now open for the Uſe of the Public, on Payment of the following Tolls, *viz.*

For all Coals entering into or going out of their Bason at Wandsworth,	*per Chaldron*,	3d.
For all other Goods entering into or going out of their Bason at Wandsworth - -	*per Ton*,	3d.

For all GOODS carried on the said RAILWAY, as follows, viz.

For Dung, - - -	*per Ton, per Mile*,	1d.
For Lime, and all Manures, (except Dung,) Lime-ſtone, Chalk, Clay, Breeze, Aſhes, Sand, Bricks, Stone, Flints, and Fuller's Earth,	*per Ton, per Mile*,	2d.
For Coals, - - -	*per Chald. per Mile*,	3d.
And, For all other Goods, -	*per Ton, per Mile*,	3d.

By ORDER of the COMMITTEE,

W. B. LUTTLY,
Clerk of the Company.

Wandsworth, June 1, 1804.

The rails of these early wagon-ways were made of wood so they wore out quite quickly. When iron became cheaper to make in the eighteenth century some rails were covered with a strip of iron to make them last longer.

This photograph shows a later stage in the making of railways. Look at the rails. What do you think they are made of? How do they differ from the rails on page 36? How do the wheels differ from the wagon wheels on page 36? Railways of this sort were usually called plateways. Write a paragraph to explain how they differed from earlier wagon-ways.

All these early railways were private lines. They usually joined coalmines to the nearest river or canal. The first public railway in the world was the Surrey Iron Railway — opened in 1803. Mark this date on your time-chart. Here is the poster announcing its tolls. Use it to discover what sort of goods they expected to carry. Does it mention passengers? What does the word 'Chaldron' mean?

The Surrey Iron Railway used L-shaped rails. The reason for this, the Company said, was that 'carriages fit for a railway may also be used in the streets of a town . . . so that every person . . . may draw his goods . . . to and from the markets and his own premises without reloading.'

The first locomotives

These horse-drawn wagons were very useful, but they were not yet a challenge to canals and stage-coaches. For this a new development was needed — the steam-powered locomotive.

Steam engines were in use in the eighteenth century but they were too big and clumsy to be used to drive a truck. One reason why these engines were so big was that they used steam at very low pressure. Try to find out why this meant that the engines had to be big.

A breakthrough was made in 1802 by Richard Trevithick, a young Cornish engineer. Trevithick designed a steam engine which used what he called 'strong steam' — steam under high pressure. This allowed him to make the engine much smaller — small enough to put on a truck. From this it was a short step to make the steam engine drive the truck.

In February 1804, the world's first steam locomotive drew a train. Above is a model of what it probably looked like. Draw it on your time-chart. It made a ten mile (16 km) journey from Penydaren Ironworks (near Merthyr Tydfil) to the Glamorganshire Canal. Although the locomotive worked quite well it was too heavy for the plateway and cracked many of the cast iron plates. Soon after this first journey its wheels were taken off and it became a fixed engine.

Trevithick had shown that a steam locomotive could pull a train. But nobody wanted to use his locomotives if it meant relaying the plateways with stronger rails. Then, during the war with Napoleon horse fodder became very expensive. Coal owners realised that steam locomotives, which used coal, would be cheaper to run than horse-drawn wagons.

In 1812, the locomotive above started work at Middleton Colliery, near Leeds. It was designed by John Blenkinsop. Look carefully at the middle wheel. The cogs on this wheel fit into slots in the rail and drive the locomotive along. Blenkinsop thought this was needed, because he had made the engine much lighter than Trevithick's. Which types of railway still use this method today? Blenkinsop's engine worked well, and soon others were being built.

This is William Hedley's 'Puffing Billy' which is now in the Science Museum in London. Notice that it has wheels with flanges. People discovered that smooth flanged wheels could grip perfectly well on rails shaped like this $\mathbb{I}$ — called edge rails. These edge rails could be made much stronger than the L-shaped plates.

George Stephenson

The Stockton and Darlington Railway

Here is the first steam locomotive that had flanged wheels and ran on edge rails. It was built in 1814 by George Stephenson, the engineer at Killingworth Colliery, in Northumberland. Stephenson had been brought up around the coalmines and had learned to mend all sorts of machines. This engine and track were a great success, and in the next seven years Stephenson's reputation grew. He told a friend: 'I will do something in coming time which will astonish all England.' In 1821 he got his chance.

At this time coal from South Durham was still being taken by road to Stockton. Because this was expensive the coal owners decided to build a canal, but later they decided to build a railway instead. Stephenson was asked to be engineer-in-charge. He persuaded the Company to build a railway which could be used by steam locomotives.

September 27th 1825 was the day for the opening procession. In this drawing pick out: Stephenson driving his new engine *Locomotion*, the crowded coal wagons, the Company's only passenger coach and the man with the flag. What is he doing? Make a drawing of this scene for your time-chart. If you can visit Darlington Station, *Locomotion* is there.

The Stockton and Darlington was the first public railway to use steam locomotives and to carry passengers. But look at this poster. What is pulling this coach? What can you discover from this about the early days of the Stockton and Darlington? At that time the railway worked just like a road or canal. Anyone could use it if he paid the tolls. Why was this difficult for the locomotive drivers?

RAPID, SAFE, AND CHEAP TRAVELLING
By the Elegant NEW RAILWAY COACH,

THE UNION,

Which will COMMENCE RUNNING on the STOCKTON and DARLINGTON RAILWAY, on MONDAY the 16th day of October, 1826,

The Liverpool and Manchester Railway

By this time the businessmen of Liverpool and
Manchester were no longer satisfied with the Bridgewater Canal which was slow and had raised its tolls
sharply. So they planned to join the two cities with a
railway, and asked George Stephenson to be the
engineer. Local land-owners strongly opposed the
scheme. Stephenson said, 'We had to take a great deal of
the survey by stealth at the time when the persons were
at dinner.'

At last Parliament gave approval and work began.
This was a much bigger job than the Stockton line.
Above you can see men at work on the most difficult
part, the huge bog called Chat Moss. Can you work out
from this picture how Stephenson solved the problem by
'floating' his line across this bog?

Before the line opened the
Company held a trial at
Rainhill, and offered a
£500 prize for the best
engine. Here is the winner
— the famous 'Rocket'.
Find out more about this
famous trial and write
your own account of it.

The railway was opened on 15th September 1830. Here is a picture of the start of the procession. On the left is a special train for the Prime Minister, the Duke of Wellington. On the right are more engines. Pick out their smoking chimneys and the large barrels behind the engines. What were these for? Notice the well-dressed visitors walking about on the lines. Later, one of these guests, William Huskisson, M.P. for Liverpool, became the first railway casualty when he fell on the line and was run over by the 'Rocket' and killed.

In spite of this accident, the railway was a great success. The company was surprised to find that most of its money came from passengers, and not from heavy goods as it had expected.

This is what the trains looked like. What differences can you see between the first- and second-class carriages?

Draw part of the first-class train for your time-chart, and write a sentence to say why this railway is important.

The railway system takes shape

Because the Liverpool and Manchester Railway was so successful, there was a rush to build other lines. Businessmen now had the confidence to plan great trunk routes to link the main cities in Britain.

Look at this picture of the inside of Kilsby Tunnel. Compare its size with that of the canal tunnel on page 29. Notice how small the men and horses look. At the top of the picture, in the shaft of sunlight, you can just see some men in a large bucket being drawn up to an opening. This is one of the sixteen working shafts from which the tunnel was bored. The tunnel is lined with bricks. 36 million of them were used, enough to make a footpath three feet (1 m) wide stretching from London to Aberdeen.

This huge tunnel was one of the major works on the London and Birmingham railway. This was the first of the main trunk lines. Work began on it in 1833 and the line was opened in 1838. Here is a portrait of the man who was appointed as chief engineer on the great work, much the biggest project ever attempted up to that time. He is George Stephenson's son, Robert, who was then 29 years old.

Robert Stephenson

Kilsby Tunnel was Robert Stephenson's greatest worry.
When the working shafts were first dug, they ran into
terrible quicksands and were completely flooded. To draw
off the water Stephenson brought in 13 steam pumps.
Together, these pumped out 1,800 gallons (8,100 litres) of
water each minute, but they had to keep pumping for a
year and a half before the quicksand was beaten and
tunnelling could begin again. Above is the scene on Kilsby
Hill. Pick out some of the pumps in front, and behind them
the machine (called a *horse gin*) for raising the bucket in
the working shaft. Can you see how this works? Make a
simple model of it with pipe-cleaners, cotton, a cotton-reel,
and two small wheels.

Here is a picture of Robert Stephenson's greatest rival as
a railway engineer — Isambard Kingdom Brunel. In 1835,
when he too was only twenty-nine, Brunel was made
engineer of the Great Western Railway. He was determined
to make this 'the finest work in England' and he certainly
succeeded. Brunel was one of the boldest engineers of the
nineteenth century, and it was the Great Western Railway
which made his reputation.

Brunel

The greatest work on this railway was the two-mile (3 km) tunnel through Box Hill. Look in your atlas to see where this is. Here is the east end of the tunnel. Notice that it is cut through solid rock and needs no brick lining to support it. Imagine this being cut by thousands of men with only picks and dynamite, working by candlelight. It took only five years, but 100 men were killed making it. It is said that on April 9th, which is Brunel's birthday, the rising sun shines through the tunnel from end to end.

The railway was opened in 1841 and after some early problems with engines it worked very well. By 1847, with new engines designed by Daniel Gooch, the trip to Bristol took just two and a half hours. Compare this with the speed of Parson Woodforde's coach to Bath 60 years earlier. The cost of a first-class ticket was 27/— and second class 18/6. Make a note of the average speed and cost per mile or kilometre for your time-chart and compare them with today's.

The speed with which the railway system took shape is amazing. Here is a map of the railways in 1852. How many years was this after the Liverpool and Manchester Railway opened?

Look carefully at the picture below and count the number of rails. The engine is running on a track with the rails laid 7 ft. (213 cm) apart. This was called the broad gauge. The middle rail marks the width of the standard gauge with rails 4 ft. 8½ ins. (144 cm) apart. The standard gauge had been used by George Stephenson at Stockton and most later railways were built to this gauge. But Brunel decided that this was too narrow for the high speeds he intended. He persuaded the Great Western to use his 'broad gauge of 7 ft'. Can you think what trouble this led to when the two systems met? In 1845, there was a contest between the two gauges, and Brunel's system won. But he was too late. Too many miles of standard gauge track had been laid already. In 1846 Parliament decided that all future railways must be standard gauge. For a time the Great Western had a third rail as in the picture. In 1892 they abandoned the broad gauge altogether.

47

The navvies

Here is a picture of George Stephenson talking to a group of *navvies* — the men who actually built the railway lines. Notice the very simple tools they have — pick, shovel and wheelbarrow. These were the tools with which the railways were built. There were hardly any machines to help, apart from steam pumping engines.

When the main railways were being built there were large 'armies' of navvies everywhere. In 1845, about 200,000 of them were at work building 3,000 miles (4,800 km) of line. Once the line had been marked out the navvies arrived. If they could not find lodgings in nearby villages they built themselves camps to live in. People were terrified of these camps, particularly after pay-day. Navvies were usually paid once a month, and for a few days afterwards they would drink and riot and fight amongst themselves.

When a job was finished, or if they got fed up, the navvies would tramp off to another line. This cartoon shows a navvy on the tramp with his equipment. Pick out:
— his pick, shovel and wheelbarrow
— lantern (for tunnel work)
— jug (for whisky or beer)
Does he have the same tools as the navvies in the top picture? The artist has shown this navvy with a sword, but they did not usually carry one. They did have strange nicknames though. One was called the Duke of Wellington because he had a nose like the Duke's. Others were called Cat's Meat, Hedgehog, Gorger, and Mary Ann.

This cartoon was published when a group of navvies was being sent
to help the army in the Crimean War. It shows what people thought
the navvies would do to the Russians. Of course, the navvies did not
really go to fight — they went to build a railway so that supplies could
get through to the army at Sebastapol. This railway, 29 miles (46 km)
long, was built in about eight weeks.

As they proved in the Crimea, the best navvies were amazing
workers. A good navvy could shift twenty tons of earth and rocks in a
day. It was dangerous work too. Thousands of navvies were killed
building the railways. Sometimes they were killed because they were
careless or reckless. On the Kilsby Tunnel three men were killed one
after another trying to jump across one of the shafts in a game of
follow my leader. No wonder ordinary people were rather frightened
of them. But it was generally thought that British navvies could out-
work anyone. So they were in great demand to build railways abroad,
in France, Italy, Canada, Latin America and Australia.

How the railways were built

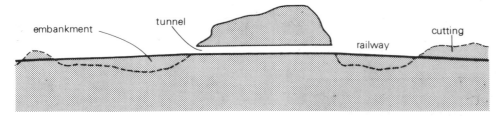

This diagram shows how the railway engineers laid out a line. Can you see the *cuttings* through the higher ground, and *embankments* to build up the level of the line through the dips? Engineers always tried to lay out a line so that the earth taken from the cuttings would be enough to make the embankments. Why was this? If there was very high ground to be passed a tunnel would be needed.

On the first main lines huge earthworks were needed because the engineers tried to lay their lines as level as possible. This was because the early engines were not powerful enough to pull well up steep hills.

Here is Tring cutting on the London and Birmingham Railway. Can you find the navvies digging out the earth? The planks laid up the side of the cutting are called barrow runs. Notice the navvies with wheelbarrows on these runs. Can you see how the barrows are being pulled up by ropes which are attached to horses at the top? This was called 'making the running' and you had to be very strong and skilful to avoid falling off the planks.

Here is how an embankment was made. Can you see the horse pulling a loaded truck on rails? These were temporary rails laid from the nearest cutting to the embankment. At the end of the rails can you see a truck which has tipped its load over the edge? The navvies had a very clever way of doing this. They made the horse gallop the final stretch and unhitched it from the truck just at the last moment. The truck then rushed on and was suddenly stopped by a piece of timber across the rails. This made the truck tip forward and the earth poured down the embankment. The horse was then hitched up again to drag the empty truck away.

When the railway had to go through solid rock, dynamite was used. Next is a picture of rocks being blasted near Linslade on the London and Birmingham. Can you see smoke rising from the rocks in front and chunks of rock being thrown into the air? Notice that the navvies are standing well back. You can imagine how dangerous this blasting was, particularly inside a tunnel. The worst job was packing dynamite into the drilled hole with a ram called a stemmer. If this struck the rock-side it could make sparks which set off the dynamite. This is what happened to one navvy named Jackson. 'He was looking over John Webb's shoulder, while he was stemming a hole charged with powder, when the blast went off, blowing the stemmer through Jackson's head and killed him on the spot.'

In this picture you can see two of the great bridges of the nineteenth century. Can you recognise the one in front? If not, look back at page 17. The one behind is the Britannia Bridge. This was designed by Robert Stephenson and takes the Holyhead railway over the Menai Straights. If you look carefully at the picture you can see most of the forms of transport which were used in the nineteenth century:
— two trains
— tiny horse-drawn coaches on the bridge
— sailing ships
— and a paddle steamer.

Here you see the Britannia Bridge being built. At first Stephenson had planned to build a suspension bridge with the railway carried in a huge iron tube. After he had made several models of this he decided that the tube could be made strong enough to support itself. The tubes were made in eight sections and those for the middle of the bridge were built on wooden pontoons at the water's edge. They were then floated out to the piers and slowly jacked up into position, while the stone supports were built up under them. Can you see how this is being done in the picture? The Britannia Bridge was finished in 1850 and was still in use in 1970, carrying trains many times the weight that Stephenson designed it for. In 1970 the bridge was damaged by fire and rebuilt to a slightly different design. Try to find out what the difference is. Make a model of this bridge in cardboard using balsawood for the piers. Mark the date of the bridge on your time-chart.

Most of the great railway bridges have stood the test of time. But occasionally there were disasters. The best known is the Tay Bridge disaster in 1879. Find out about this and write an account of it.

Comfort on the railway

Look again at the Liverpool and Manchester trains on page 43. Notice that the first-class coaches look like stage-coach bodies stuck together and put on wheels. This became the common pattern for first-class carriages. Here is the inside of a first-class carriage in the 1840s. Notice the upholstered seats, arm rests and head rests. Do you see where the gentleman in the middle has put his top hat? These carriages were very comfortable, though it was not usual for there to be lavatories on trains even for first-class passengers until the late 1870s.

Here is a photograph of an early third-class compartment from the Stockton and Darlington railway. Notice the wooden seats and lack of windows. You can just see the hole in the roof where the oil lamp went. There was no heating in trains like this, and lavatories were not provided for third-class passengers until the very end of the nineteenth century.

REFRESHMENT ROOMS.

THE MOMENT THE TRAIN ARRIVES AT WOLVERTON, RUSH TO THE REFRESHMENT ROOM LIKE THE WHIRLWIND.

AND IMMEDIATELY SIEZE A PORK PIE

IF YOU ARE FOOLISH, HAVE A GLASS OF HOT BRANDY AND WATER, WHICH WILL BEGIN TO COOL JUST AS THE BELL RING FOR DEPARTURE.

BUT IF YOU ARE WISE, YOU WILL HAVE A PINT BOTTLE OF CREAMY STOUT, WHICH YOU WILL HAVE TIME TO DRINK WITH DIGNIFIED GUSTO.

REFRESHMENT ROOMS

WARM YOURSELF AT THE STOVE BEFORE YOU GO

PAY FOR YOUR REFRESHMENT, OF COURSE IF YOU HAVE TIME.

IF YOU HAVE NOT.

WHY.

SO MUCH THE WORSE FOR THE REFRESHMENT ROOM

AND SO MUCH THE BETTER FOR YOU

FOR THE INFORMATION OF YOUNG GENTLEMEN ADDICTED TO FLIRTING WITH YOUNG LADIES, IT IS AS WELL TO REMARK THAT .

At first the railway companies had not been very interested in providing cheap travel for ordinary people. But in 1844 the Government passed a law which made all companies provide at least one train for third-class passengers each day. These trains had to give protection from the weather, and had to average 12 miles (19 km) per hour. The fare was a penny a mile. As you can see from the picture opposite, these carriages were not very comfortable but trains like this did allow cheap travel for the first time. You can see some early carriages like this at the York Railway Museum.

Dining cars were provided only late in the nineteenth century. At certain stations, where the train stopped for a few minutes, you could dash to the refreshment room for some food. These drawings come from a humorous guide-book which gave passengers tips about what to do on the railway. Invent some cartoons yourself which would tell people how to be comfortable on these early trains.

What effect did the railways have?

Look at this picture. Can you see the stage-coach which has been abandoned in the courtyard? In the 1840s this happened to most of the coaching business on main roads. Why do you think the railways were so successful in taking passengers from the stage-coaches? Of course coaches were still needed where there were no railways and there were also many horse-drawn carriages in towns until the motor car arrived.

The canals lost business to the railways too. A number of them were bought up by railway companies. Many others had to close.

The mail business went to the railways as well. Soon there were special vans like this one in which the mail could be sorted on the journey. What do you think the large net on the side is for?

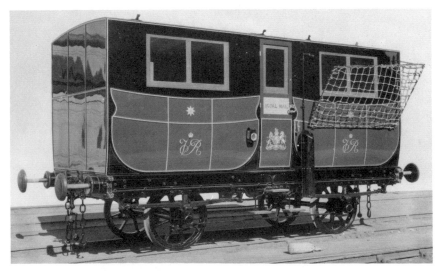

Cheap travel allowed ordinary people to move about freely for the first time. Millions paid their first visit to London to see the Great Exhibition (1851). 'Excursion trains' allowed working people to have special outings. Most important were the cheap 'workmen's trains' which the railway had to run. Here is one of these trains arriving at Victoria Station, London in 1865. Notice that the lights are on because it is very early in the morning. Can you tell what sort of jobs any of these people did from the tools they are carrying? With trains like this people could get out of the crowded city centres and live in the suburbs. Before, they had had to live within walking distance of their work.

In London, underground trains helped to solve the problem of traffic jams. The first was the Metropolitan Railway which opened in 1863.

Steamships

In 1835, at a meeting of directors of the Great Western Railway, someone said how very long their railway was going to be. 'Why not make it longer,' said Brunel, 'and have a steamboat go from Bristol to New York and call it the *Great Western*?' In this way, the Atlantic liner was born.

Successful steamboats had been built before steam locomotives, and by the time Brunel spoke there were quite a number of paddle-steamers working on Britain's rivers and round her coast. But people thought that an ocean-going steamboat was impossible to build because it could not carry enough coal for an ocean crossing. Brunel thought this was nonsense.

Work began on the *Great Western* in 1836 and two years later she was ready. Here she is on her first trip to New York. Notice that she is driven by huge paddle wheels. Brunel had hoped that his ship would be the first to steam across the Atlantic but she was just beaten to New York by the tiny *Sirius*. However the *Great Western* crossed in only fifteen days and arrived with plenty of coal. Brunel had been quite right about steamships. Draw a picture of the *Great Western* on your time-chart.

No sooner had the *Great Western* proved herself than Brunel began to plan an even bigger and better ship. This time he decided to make the hull of iron and not of oak, and to use the new screw propeller instead of paddles. Here is this new ship, called the *Great Britain*, just after her launching at Bristol in 1843. She became the first iron-hulled liner to cross the Atlantic. Mark this date on your chart. The strength of this iron hull was shown dramatically in 1846 when she went aground in Dundrum Bay in Ireland. She lay on this stormy shore for nearly a year before being refloated and repaired. In fact this amazing ship still exists today. After lying beached in the Falkland Islands for many years, in 1970 she was towed back to her original dock in Bristol where you can look over her.

Steamships had one great advantage over sailing ships. Can you think what this was? But until a more efficient engine became available in the 1860s, steamships had to waste too much valuable cargo space carrying their own coal supply. For this reason the great sailing ships called 'clippers' were able to compete on the long voyages from Australia and China until the 1870s. You can visit the most famous clipper, the *Cutty Sark*, in dry dock at Greenwich in London.

The 'Great Eastern'

In 1854 work began on Brunel's most fantastic project — the *Great Eastern*. She was to be the largest ship in the world, twice the size of the *Great Britain*, with a length of 680 feet (204 metres). Because of her enormous length, she was built parallel with the river at Millwall in London, and had to be launched sideways.

Here is Brunel on the day of her launching, and below is the scene at the Napier Yard. Notice the two huge wooden cradles in which the hull was meant to slide down the slipway. Behind them, wound on enormous drums, are the chains to hold her steady as she slipped. At first, the ship would not move, and Brunel ordered the special rams to start pushing. Immediately, the front end of the ship slid a little way. The ground trembled and many of the spectators were terrified. The back end also slid a short distance. As it did so, a taughtening chain made a winch handle spin round, smashing the legs of an old labourer who was standing on it for a better view. The launching was abandoned, and some hours later the poor man died.

Over the next three months the great ship was slowly pushed towards the water. In the end Brunel had eighteen rams pushing against the hull. At last, on January 31st 1858, the ship was floated off at high tide.

The overwork and worry, particularly over money, of building and launching this great ship helped to kill Brunel, and he died before her first voyage to New York. Here she is on that trip. Notice the huge paddle wheels and the sails. The *Great Eastern* was the only ship ever to be built with both paddles and screw propeller.

In spite of her size the *Great Eastern* was not a success. She had cost too much to build and her engines were not powerful enough, although at that time they were much the biggest ever built. When the Suez Canal was opened in 1869 she was too big to go through and so was not used on the Far Eastern trade for which she was designed. But her great size did make her ideal for laying underwater cables. Brunel, at least, would have been pleased if he had lived to see her lay the first cable under the Atlantic in 1866. Messages could be sent instantly from Britain to America via this cable. Mark the date on your time-chart. Can you now make a list of all the ways in which communications had improved since the postboy on his horse in the early eighteenth century?

Things to do

Look at the map on the opposite page and find where you would see:
— the *Cutty Sark* and the National Maritime Museum,
— a flight of 29 locks,
— a flight of 30 locks,
— the Anderton Lift,
— the Tay Bridge,
— *Locomotion*,
— the *Great Britain*,
— the Foxton Staircase,
— the Pont Cysyllte Aqueduct,
— the Harecastle Tunnel,
— the Clifton Suspension Bridge.

   Make a list of museums dealing with railways and other forms of transport. Is there one near your school?

   As well as going to some of the places listed on the map, you may be able to find other interesting remains of the Transport Revolution in your area. Look for tollhouses, bridges, canals and railway stations. Try to find out when they were built and why. You may find information to help your study in your library.

   Write notes about:
— travellers in the eighteenth century,
— early roads and the work of two famous road-builders,
— mail-coaches,
— canals,
— locomotives and the early railways,
— the first transatlantic steamships.

   Make models of the various kinds of transport you have shown on your time-chart and write notes about each one.

   . . This book does not cover automobiles, air transport or space travel. Find out about these from other books and make a time-chart to record your findings.

Some places and museums to visit

Caledonian Canal

Crinan Canal

Tay Bridge
(Dundee)

Edinburgh
Royal Scottish
Museum
Transport Museum

Forth Road and
Rail Bridges

Glasgow
Museum of Transport

Royal Border Bridge
(Berwick-upon-Tweed)

Newcastle
High Level Bridge
Museum of Science & Engineering

Belfast
Transport
Museum

Carlisle
Citadel Station

Locomotion
(Darlington)

York
Railway
Museum

Hull
Maritime and
Transport Museums

Sankey
Viaduct

Lune Aqueduct
(Lancaster)

Anderton Lift
(Northwich)

Menai Bridge

Bridgewater Canal

Manchester Ship Canal

Crich, Derbyshire
Tramway Museum

Britannia
Rail Bridge

Penrhyn Castle
Museum

Birmingham
Museum of Science
and Industry

Portmadoc
Ffestiniog
Railway Museum

Harecastle Tunnel
(Kidsgrove)

Towyn
Narrow Gauge
Railway Museum

Pont Cysyllte Aqueduct
(Llangollen)

Foxton Staircase
(Market Harborough)

**Stoke
Bruerne, Northants**
Waterways Museum

Flight of 30 locks
(Tardebigge)

Kilsby Tunnel

Blisworth Tunnel

London
Science Museum
(S. Kensington)

Museum of British
Transport
(Clapham)

National Maritime
Museum
(Greenwich)

Severn Road Bridge

Swindon
Great Western
Railway Museum

Tring Cutting
Maidenhead
Bridge

Clifton Suspension Bridge

S. S. Great Britain
(Bristol Docks)

Flight of 29 locks
(Devizes)

Cutty Sark
(Greenwich)

Maidstone
Tyrrwhitt-Drake
Museum of Carriages

Brighton Station

Tamar
Bridge

63

Index